OMNIBUS PRESS PRESENTS

'N SYNC
'N Detail

This book is an updated edition of Omnibus Press Presents
The Story of 'N Sync by Ashley Adams originally published in May 1999.

Copyright © 2000 Omnibus Press
(A Division of Book Sales Limited)

Written by: Ashley Adams
Cover/Book Design: Jade Romigin

US ISBN: 0.8256.1801.0
UK ISBN: 0.7119.8385.7

Exclusive distributors:
Book Sales Limited
8/9 Frith Street,
London W1V 5TZ, UK

Music Sales Corporation
257 Park Avenue South
New York City, NY 10010, USA

Music Sales PTY, Ltd
120 Rothschild Avenue
Roseberry, NSW 2018
Australia

To the Music Trade only:
Music Sales Limited,
8/9 Frith Street,
London W1V 5TZ, UK

Photo Credits:
Bob Berg/ Retna Limited, USA:
Bernhard Kunndtedt/ Retna Ltd/ Retna Pictures:
6, 9,10,13,14,17,18,19, 21, 22, 26,
27, 28, 29, 34, 36, 38, 41, 42, 43, 48
Bill Davila/ London Features International: 55(Joey)
Gregg DeGuirel/ London Features International: 55(JC),
61(bottom), 63(middle), 63(bottom)
Melanie Edwards/ Retna Limited, USA: 39, 63(top)
Steve Granitz/ Retna Limited: 25 top
Tim Hale/ Retna Limited, USA: 3, 4, 5
Jen Lowery: 7, 25 bottom, 33, 37, 45
Michael Schreiber/ Retna Limited, USA: 61(middle)
Kelly Swift: 25 middle, 30 top, 30 middle
Dennis Van Tine/ London Features International: 55(Justin), 55(Chris), 61(top),
Frank White: Title Page, 47, 55(Lance)
Ron Wolfson/ London Features International: 54, 59, 64

Front Cover Photograph: Ron Wolfson/ London Features International
Back Cover Photograph: Melanie Edwards/ Retna Pictures
Printed in the United States of America by Vicks Lithograph and Printing Corp.

'N Sync is one of the hottest groups of the late Nineties—and with their endless energy and talent, they promise to be one of the top musical acts of the new millennium. Justin Timberlake; J.C. Chasez; Chris Kirkpatrick; Joey Fatone, Jr.; and Lance Bass have taken the international pop scene by storm with their irresistible blend of five-part harmonies, beautiful melodies, catchy dance beats, and unforgettable live shows.

They may be young, but 'N Sync are no newcomers to the entertainment world. All five members of this group have quite a list of credits to their names—including movies, stage and television shows, *The Mickey Mouse Club,* and much more. And all this before the fateful day in 1995 when they all came together in Orlando, Florida to form 'N Sync! Practice, dedication, and a very "in sync" vibe soon paid off, and the group was off to Europe to record their debut album and take off on the roller coaster ride of a lifetime.

Today 'N Sync have two multiplatinum U.S. albums, *'N Sync* and *Home for Christmas,* and a third on the way. Their singles "I Want You Back," "Tearin' Up My Heart," and "(God Must Have Spent) A Little More Time on You" have topped the charts worldwide. Their high-energy concerts sell out night after night. But they still take time before every single show to meet a new group of fans. The secret to 'N Sync's success is that they don't do it for the fame and fortune—they do it all for their fans.

'N Sync is a dream of a group, and so it makes sense that they came together in a land of fantasy. Chris Kirkpatrick, an energetic young performer at Universal Studios in Orlando, Florida, had an idea that grew and grew while he was busy singing and dancing his days away. He wanted to put together a musical group that could blend five-part harmonies with upbeat pop and present it all with the entertainment sensibility he'd learned onstage at the theme park. Chris would describe the Orlando scene years later to MTV's John Norris in a December 4, 1998, interview, saying, "It really is a melting pot of talent because there's so much music, theater, so much opportunities. It really is a small town because everybody knows each other because of the business."

Chris broached the subject of his concept to fourteen-year-old Justin Timberlake, whom he had met during auditions. Chris had heard Justin sing, and had recognized the kind of talent that would help his dream become a reality. Justin, although barely a teenager, was no newcomer to the entertainment world and had earned his stripes on television as one of the cast of Disney's new version of *The Mickey Mouse Club*. Justin liked the idea of forming a band, and quickly enlisted fellow former mouseketeer J.C. Chasez, whose soulful voice was a perfect complement to Justin's funky style and Chris's soprano. Years later, J.C. was full of good things to say about the *MMC* during 'N Sync's America Online chat. "I would say that it was the experience of a lifetime," he raved. "We got to do all spectrums of the business, not just singing and dancing, but acting too. It's something that will be with us for the rest of our lives, it was a great experience."

It wasn't long before Joey Fatone, a Brooklyn native, fell into the fold. Joey, a charismatic performer with a love of doo-wop, had shared the stage with Chris in Universal's *Beetlejuice Graveyard Revue*, and knew J.C. through some of his own high school pals who had also been on the *MMC*. The guys were ready to rumble, but they were missing a key ingredient: a bass voice to round out the mix and complete the harmony.

JUST DO IT
SUN STUDIO

Justin picked up the phone and contacted his former vocal coach back home in Memphis, Tennessee, to see if he might be able to suggest anyone. And that is how Lance Bass, a day-care worker in Clinton, Mississippi, found himself on a plane to Florida to meet up with the foursome who wanted to be a fivesome. As soon as they all met, the guys knew they had the perfect mix of voices . . . and personalities!

They set to work practicing and putting together an act. They spent hours each day working on what would soon become one of the hottest bands to hit the charts. They rehearsed whenever and wherever they could, often juggling time in between their day jobs and singing into the wee hours of the morning. It didn't take them long to realize they were on to something good. But they needed one more thing: a name. Justin's mother complimented the fledgling group on how in sync they were vocally, and later as she was fooling around with the letters of the boys names, trying to come up with a name for the band, she discovered that the guys really were 'N Sync. The last letters of the members first names (using Lance's nickname Lansten) formed a band name everyone agreed was ace. It was time to giddy up!

The unknown 'N Sync crew knew they needed to get the attention of someone in the entertainment industry with some clout, and so they decided to do something a little different. Instead of sending out demo tapes like every other wannabe group, they recorded a video demo package, wisely realizing that their energy, dancing skills, and above all their ability to entertain were an important part of their appeal. They printed their own posters, chose their own wardrobe, worked out their own choreography, and sent the demo—which included a cover version of the Beatles' hit "We Can Work It Out"—out into the world.

And work it out they did. When the band first formed, Justin would years later recall to *Entertainment Weekly* in its March 5, 1999, cover story on 'N Sync, "We'd perform for whoever would listen. We'd be in the middle of a restaurant saying, 'Can we sing for you?'" A year after 'N Sync was born—a year full of performing anywhere, anyhow, and honing their skills—their demo package grabbed the attention of an entrepreneur named Louis Pearlman.

Lou Pearlman made his first couple of million through launching an aviation company that flew top business executives from the airport into New York City in helicopters, so that they wouldn't have to waste time sitting in traffic in a stretch limo. He came into contact with the grandfather of the boy bands, New Kids on the Block, when the group chartered one of his jets. The businessman couldn't believe that these "Kids" were successful enough to afford his services, and picked up the phone to call his cousin, Art Garfunkel of Simon & Garfunkel fame, to get an insider's scoop on the young upstarts. Pearlman had always had a love of music, and years later, with the memory of the New Kids in his mind, he decided to take none other than the Backstreet Boys under his wing with former New Kids tour manager Johnny Wright.

'N Sync joined up with Pearlman and Wright, and signed a recording deal with BMG Germany. Wait a minute, you might say—why Germany? Well, back in 1996 pop wasn't the sound of the moment in the United States. Grunge, punk, and alternative ruled the airwaves, and five clean-cut pop stars who could sing *a cappella* and dance like pros just weren't the ticket. Johnny Wright realized that in order to record the kind of album 'N Sync should record, they had to do it in Europe. He also knew that the band could develop their act and hopefully become very popular in the more pop-orientated musical climate abroad.

Lance later explained to *Entertainment Weekly Online* why the band went all the way across the Atlantic Ocean to start their career, saying, "In Europe there's just an abundance of groups and soloists. They have maybe four times as many of everything. They have four Mariah Careys, four Backstreet Boys. And they love everybody.

That's why everyone kind of goes to try out new stuff. Even now, Michael Jackson and Madonna release their material first in Europe before they bring it here, just to kind of see what it's going to do."

So it was that the 'N Sync five landed in recording studios in Hamburg, Munich, and in Stockholm, Sweden's Cheiron Studios. Joey would later tell *Billboard* in its March 20, 1999, issue, "We liked the sound that producers like Denniz Pop and Max Martin were doing," adding, "They have an original sound . . . a very full, upbeat Swedish pop sound that we like." Pop, Martin, and Kristian Lundin–the Swedish producers and writers behind "I Want You Back" and "Tearin' Up My Heart"–have also put hits together for the likes of the Backstreet Boys, U.K. sensation Five, and fellow Scandinavians Robyn and Ace of Base.

But what made 'N Sync stand out in such a busy European music scene? Why did they make it so big, so fast, in Germany, Austria, Switzerland, and Sweden? Johnny Wright told *Billboard* in its March 20, 1999, issue, "Many of the big teen acts at the time in Germany were not singing live. They were all lip-syncing. And 'N Sync wasn't. They can sing. So they would always sing songs *a cappella*, as well as with music. It was important that they not come across as another one of those manufactured poster boy acts." Jan Bolz, the managing director of BMG Ariola Munich, emphasized in *Billboard* that 'N Sync had something special, saying, "We could not have done this with a German band. Americans are great entertainers."

By the way, the idea to use the * in the *'N Sync* logo came from a very unusual source. The band met up with psychic Uri Geller while they were in the U.K., and he reportedly advised the guys to put a star on their record to ensure its success–looks like it worked! That's one psychic I'd carry on consulting.

'N Sync, the album, was first released in Europe in May 1997. The first single "I Want You Back" was already riding high on the German charts. Ready or not, the time had come for 'N Sync to take off on the roller coaster ride of their lives. Little did they know it was destined to last a long, long time with barely a chance to catch their breaths. The hot new group toured for the next two years in Europe, Asia, South Africa, and Mexico with Justin's mother Lynn and Lance's mother Diane (an English teacher) as tour chaperones. "We took care of them, fussed at them if they weren't getting enough rest or food," Diane reminisced to *People Online* in its February 8, 1999, issue. "It was exhausting." Exhausting, but energizing at the same time. 'N Sync knew they had what it took to conquer their homeland, and the time was right–America was tired of alternative, and ready for gold old-fashioned talent and a bit of fun. Groups like the Backstreet Boys and the Spice Girls had knocked on the door, and the welcome mat was out for the return of pop.

The U.S. *'N Sync* album was released in America in March 1998 on RCA, and featured a different track listing than its European counterpart, including some extra tracks that were recorded in studios in New York and at Trans Continental Studios in Orlando. Trans Continental, today the headquarters of Lou Pearlman and Johnny Wright, is located just down the road from Sea World. Nowadays, there is definitely a unique vibe at Trans Con. The Los Angeles *Times* January 24, 1999, article by Geoff Boucher entitled "The Making of Heartthrobs Inc." noted that the Orlando office "is inevitably described by everyone involved as a family-style workplace far removed from the cutthroat music industry hubs of Los Angeles and New York," and quoted executive Jay Marose as saying, "It took me a few weeks to get used to everyone hugging each other in the halls." Trans Continental has a few more pop acts up its sleeve, ready to hit the road and the charts, namely C Note, Take 5, Lyte Funkie Ones, and girl band Innosense.

But back to 'N Sync's American debut. The band enjoyed their fair share of success at first, but it wasn't the same as the stardom and fame they had become accustomed to in Europe. In fact, it was a relief of sorts to be able to walk down the street without being recognized, and the guys reveled in a bit of normality in between gigs, radio promotions, and magazine interviews with major music industry magazines as well as top teen publications. "I Want You Back" hit the singles chart, and the video began to be played more and more frequently on MTV. 'N Sync joined the likes of Mariah Carey, Paula Cole, Olivia Newton-John, and Matchbox 20 for a benefit concert at Radio City Music Hall on May 31; the concert's proceeds went to PAX, a non-profit organization that tries to put a stop to gun violence in America. This wasn't the band's first—nor would it be the last—piece of charity work. 'N Sync performed at Charity '98 in Oberhausen, Germany, to raise funds for sick children. They were featured on a charity single called "Children Need a Helping Hand" which was a Number One hit on the German charts.

'N Sync took to the road on a full-on North American tour which began on the Fourth of July in St. Petersburg, Florida, and went on to touch down in many Canadian cities, as well as dates at Chicago's House of Blues, the Warner Theatre in Washington D.C., and the Kansas State Fair. The sound of 'N Sync was beginning to take a grip on the U.S. As Johnny Wright told *Billboard* in its March 20, 1999, issue, "The European producers were creating something fresh and new. And Americans supported it. It was a clean-cut sound. And the act supported that. Parents liked it, too. So the sound took off here, too. In Europe, it wasn't a new sound, it was just pop music." Although the 'N Sync five didn't take the States by storm the moment they stepped off the plane, it wouldn't be long before they were to become a major sensation.

It was the July 18, 1998, "'N Sync In Concert" Disney special, however, that really broke the ice. The concert was originally supposed to be a Backstreet Boys special, but just two weeks before the scheduled taping, Backstreet backed out of the gig, and 'N Sync were only too happy to take the slot. "Even after we filmed it, we just thought it was a little concert," Chris told *Entertainment Weekly* in its March 5, 1999, cover story. "I was like, 'Well, that was cool. Now we gotta

go work on our *careers*." Barely a month after the concert, *'N Sync* the album rocketed its way right into the Top Ten. And there it would stay for a long, long time. At the beginning of August 1998 'N Sync's album broke into the *Billboard* charts at Number Nine, one place below the Backstreet Boys who were at Number Eight, and one slot above none other than Will Smith.

'N Sync the album was a gold mine of the many musical strengths of the group. The opening track, "Tearin Up My Heart," was destined to be a major hit. Aside from the song's catchy melody and

irresistible beat, the lyrics (*It's tearin' up my heart, When I'm with you / And when we are apart, I feel it too / And no matter what I do I feel the pain / With or without you*) are a perfect testament to the anguish of young love. As J.C. said in the *'N the Mix* official home video, "Believe it or not, there's a great message in the song that I think everybody can relate to." Joey describes it in simple terms, as a "knot–butterflies in your stomach." And we've all been there. The album also offers some sweet love songs. "(God Must Have Spent) A Little More Time on You" is a standout track, and you'll find that all of the band members cite it as one of their favorites. Its heartfelt lyrics (*In all of creation, all things great and small / You are the one who surpasses them all*) are a joy to sing. As Justin says on the *'N Sync* Enhanced CD, the song "relates to me a lot just because I'm a very spiritual person." He explains, "I think it's a wittier way of saying to someone how special they are." "For the Girl Who Has Everything" is another sweet ballad. As Joey says in the *'N the Mix* official home video, "Being in love–it's a gift, and a special gift. You can't put a price on it."

The thirteen songs showcase the five-strong singing force of 'N Sync's many vocal styles and ranges. Their harmonizing is, of course, a constant strength. "You Got It" is a beat-driven dance track with a smattering of street-corner doo-wop thrown in. A Stevie Wonder influence can be heard on "I Just Wanna Be with You" and "Everything I Own" brings Michael Jackson to mind at times.

Lance told *Entertainment Weekly Online* in its October 20, 1998, article entitled "Tearin' Up the Charts" about the cover song "Sailing," which was originally a hit by Christopher Cross. "It's just one of those songs that you've always loved, but if you tried to name the artist you probably couldn't. We didn't know who sang it when we first decided to do it." The band felt the song would be "vocally challenging" with its many parts, and as Lance went on to say, "So we did it almost two years ago and it's been our baby since. It's been like our pride and joy."

The album closes with the only song the band helped to write, "Giddy Up." It's the funkiest track by far, featuring the sound of an old scratched record. Chris described "Giddy Up" during his January 5, 1999, Yahoo chat, saying, "It's about having fun. Getting off your butt and have fun. That's pretty much the theme of the song." It's a fitting conclusion to an album that would prove that 'N Sync planned to have a lot of fun in their own country.

'N Sync rounded off the summer with a few choice appearances, to say the least. The band had a fantastic time on August 28 helping multimillionaire and entrepreneur Richard Branson promote the opening of his new Virgin Megastore in New York City's Union Square. The band joined British songstress Petula Clark (who had the boys sing along with her hit "Downtown") on top of a red London double-decker bus. The party drove through the streets of the city, delighting expectant fans and surprised New Yorkers alike, and Richard Branson's trademark grin seemed even wider than usual when 'N Sync got the crowds going. And they certainly know how to do that. Cheerleader-style chants rev up the audience to the tune of "When I say "'N" y'all say "Sync"–"N!" . . . "SYNC!" . . . "'N!" . . . "SYNC!" It's hard for the boys to resist playing with the crowd, and Justin has been known to shout out the command, "Now scream!" to tremendous effect. 'N Sync also performed at the Miss Teen USA pageant, and appeared on the *Tonight Show with Jay Leno* on September 10 along with *Ally McBeal* star Calista Flockhart. They finished off the month with a spot on MTV's *Total Request Live*, much to the delight of the horde of screaming fans outside the Times Square, New York City, studio.

On October 14, 'N Sync were pinching themselves as they set out on tour with one of their favorite artists, Janet Jackson. In an October 6 *MTV News* interview, Chris raved about the opportunity to be a part of Janet's Velvet Rope tour, saying, "We don't care if we get booed off the stage. We're just gonna be like, 'What's up Janet. You're welcome. They're ready for you.'" Needless to say, the band did not get booed off the stage. On Yahoo, Lance described Janet Jackson as "one of the nicest persons in the world . . . very down to earth and humble." Joey has admitted to having a crush on her! One of the highlights of the tour was the 'N Sync and Janet *a cappella* duet of Stevie Wonder's "Overjoyed." In addition to the band's admiration for Janet's talent and professionalism, the stint on her tour gave them a chance to warm up for their very own headlining tour.

But first: a few more TV appearances, including a November 4 German chart show and a November 6 *Tonight Show with Jay Leno*, this time with Courtney Thorne-Smith. The band's favorite television experience? Has to be the Rosie O'Donnell show. Lance raved about 'N Sync's appearance on the daytime talk show during his February 22, 1999, Yahoo chat, saying, "It was great. It was a dream come true. As everyone knows, she is like my favorite person in the world. I was really looking forward to doing it and it was everything I hoped for and more. And she surprised me by bringing in Lucy Arnez, because as she knows, my favorite actress is Lucille Ball."

'N Sync kicked off the tour, literally, at the Honolulu, Hawaii, Oia football championship pregame concert at the Aloha Stadium. 'N Sync sang the national anthem to more than 15,000 people that night. Fittingly, the official start of their tour was on November 17 in the band's hometown, Orlando, Florida, with a hot new artist as their opening act: a young lady named Britney Spears whose album . . . *Baby One More Time* was soon to make a huge dent in the charts. Britney was no stranger to at least part of the band: she had been the youngest Mouseketeer on *The Mickey Mouse Show* when Justin and J.C. were wearing their ears. So, it was a reunion of sorts. Rumors started flying that Justin and Britney were dating, but both pop stars laughed it off, claiming to be more like brother and sister than boyfriend and girlfriend.

'N Sync teamed up with the Backstreet Boys to record a benefit single released in November called "Let the Music Heal Your Soul," the work of a team of vocal artists who adopted the name Bravo All Stars. A charity organization called the Nordoff-Robbins Music Therapy Foundation was to receive the proceeds in order to help autistic and disabled kids.

Inevitably, there is a lot of hype about competition between the Backstreet Boys and 'N Sync, but the guys in 'N Sync say that's just what it is: hype. "There's no animosity," Johnny Wright insisted in the November 1998 issue of *Teen People*. "The more vocal groups there are, the better it is, because the more variety (the fans) have, the more great music they could

have." Of course, the fact that 'N Sync shared the common thread of Louis Pearlman and Johnny Wright helped fuel the comparisons between the two groups. Justin told *Teen People*, "When we put our group together–and we were together for about six months before we met Johnny–I didn't even know who the Backstreet Boys were." When the Backstreet Boys let Johnny Wright go as their manager, rumors abounded that it was because of 'N Sync's success that BSB didn't want to work with Johnny anymore. "It could have been over us; it could have been over money. I'd rather not know," J.C. told the Los Angeles *Times*. "It's none of my business." Journalists especially liked to hold the two bands up against one another. The Los Angeles *Times*, in its January 7, 1999, issue, gave a rather jaded review of the band's Universal Amphitheatre concert comparing the fivesome to BSB: "Judging from the intensity of the teen screams throughout 'N Sync's official L.A. concert debut, 'N Sync has successfully challenged the swoony sovereignty of the Backstreet Boys," columnist Natalie Nichols wrote, adding, "And they've done it largely by following the same formula."

Regardless, both groups are on top of the world, and Johnny Wright is just the right fit for 'N Sync. As a manager, he gives his all, and expects the same of his acts. As he told *Entertainment Weekly*, "I'm lucky to have acts that are hungry. I tell them straight up: When that window's open, you have to put whatever you got through it -and let's not be worried about vacations and all this other stuff." He described his very hands-on approach, saying, "I'm the artist-development person; I'm the guy who swept the teddy bears off the stage. . . . When I walk out with 'N Sync, the fans know who Johnny Wright is."

On November 10 the band's very own Christmas album entitled *Home for Christmas* was released. As any 'N Sync fan knows, the guys in the band are crazy about Christmas; and, as if the album wasn't enough of a gift to their fans, they also put out their own book, *'N Sync: The Official Book*, and their own official home video called *'N the Mix* on the very same day. *Home for Christmas* features both traditional Christmas songs, including "O Holy Night" which the band sings a cappella, "The Christmas Song (Chestnuts Roasting on an Open Fire," and "The First Noel," as well as many original tracks. It was recorded mainly at Trans Continental Studios, as well as Pennsylvania's Get Wild Studios, New York's The Loft, Los Angeles's Larrabee North Studios, Nashville's The Hot Closet, and even as far afield as FM Studio in Frankfurt, Germany. Justin and J.C. share writing credits on the single "Merry Christmas, Happy Holidays," a song whose video debuted on MTV on November 29. Christmas spirit fills the video, which features the guys riding a sleigh (with Joey at the helm) and feeding the homeless. It also includes a cameo appearance by Gary Coleman, who plays an elf! "Not just anybody can put out a Christmas record," J.C. told *Teen People* in its November 1998 cover story on the band. "(You) have to have somewhat of a following for people to want to pick it up. And that made us feel very good."

But before Christmas comes Thanksgiving, and 'N Sync celebrated the holiday in style, joining Macy's famous Thanksgiving Day parade, along with fellow musical celebrities Chicago and Monica. Lance couldn't get over being a part of the tradition he had watched every year on his grandmother's TV. The band, accompanied on their float by a giant yellow M&M, braved the weather with fur-lined hoods and clear umbrellas.

December was a busy, busy month for the 'N Sync five. How they ever had time to do their Christmas shopping we will never know. The band joined Shania Twain, Edwin McCain, the Goo Goo Dolls, Boyz II Men, Monica, Lauryn Hill, Eagle-Eye Cherry, the Bryan Setzer Orchestra, Barenaked Ladies, Shawn Mullins, and 98° at the annual Jingle Ball concert at Radio City Music Hall. The concert is sponsored by New York City radio station Z-100, and it is all in the name of fun and a very good cause. The proceeds from the show go to charity groups Share, the Refugee Project, and the Lupus Foundation of America. All of the participating groups put on a good show, and Barenaked Ladies earned a few extra squeals from the audience when they made a joke about having caught a peak at 'N Sync in the buff in the changing room. They also appeared on *Regis & Kathie Lee*, *The Disney Christmas Show*, and in *Walt Disney World's Very Merry Christmas Parade*.

All of this while their tour went on! The band did take a two-week

break to spend some time with family and friends during the holiday season, but got right back on stage two days after Christmas.

So what did the guys get for Christmas? More than a few awards, that's for sure. The band (all except J.C.) got 'N Sync-inspired tattoos late one night after being presented with their first Platinum album live on Canadian television. "I Want You Back" won Best Dance Clip and Best Dance New Artist Clip at the Billboard Music Video Awards. 'N Sync presented the Bee Gees with a Lifetime Achievement Award at the 1998 Billboard Music Awards held December 7, 1998, at the MGM Grand in Las Vegas. They also served as presenters and winners alike at the American Music Awards where they handed an award over to Garth Brooks and picked one up for Best New Artist. The band didn't do too badly at the America Online Entertainment Asylum's "You've Got Fans" online awards, in which they won CD of the Year and Favorite Musical Artist; Justin won two awards all on his own: Hottest Male and Sexiest Newcomer! In just one week in December, both their debut and Christmas albums were in the Top Ten at the same time, and the two albums combined sold 400,000 copies in only seven days. All in all, the understatement of the decade is that it was a pretty good year for the boys.

'N Sync started the New Year off with a bang, playing to a sold-out crowd in the party city of the world, Las Vegas. They now had hot new girl band B*Witched, straight from Ireland, as their support act, and the show was better than ever. As Justin said during a Yahoo chat, "You can imagine them on St. Patrick's Day. They're sweet girls. . . . Every opening act we've had has been a joy to work with."

The band showed their seemingly endless supply of energy and their love for touring when they set out on yet another full-on tour with new support act Tatyana Ali. Starting off once again in Florida, the boys hit the road with performances scheduled for almost every night in March, April, and May, playing cities in dozens of states. This time they brought a new pal on the road with them—Chris's dog, a pug named Busta.

The New York *Times* March 17, 1999, review of the Nassau Coliseum concert by columnist Ann Powers was complimentary of the band's showmanship. It said, "'N Sync evoked a different sort of entertainment: the Broadway-style revue. Like rock-and-roll, this show linked back to the circus and the vaudeville hall, but it was much more stylized and blatantly spectacular than rock."

So what exactly is it about the 'N Sync live experience that makes their concerts so special? And how do they remain in sync onstage every night, and on the road every day? The guys pride themselves on working very hard to fulfill their goal of keeping the audience entertained from the moment the show begins. The nonstop energy of 'N Sync's live show is an experience the band's fans won't soon forget.

'N Sync's fantastic dance routines are the result of teamwork—they do use professional choreographers, but the five performers contribute their own steps and ideas to the mix. As anyone who has been lucky enough to see 'N Sync live in concert can tell you, the collaboration definitely works. They make it look easy on stage because they've put so much time and effort into preparing themselves. "I was the worst dancer when I joined the group!" Lance confessed during his online Yahoo chat session on December 2, 1998. "I spent hours with a choreographer every day so I could learn." The guys still spend eight to ten hours a day before they go on tour perfecting their moves, and brush up before each concert at the sound check. In fact, although all of the guys have buff bods and are obviously in great physical shape, none of them work out—they get more than enough exercise performing!

The guys add their very own special touches to their ever-changing choreography, including ultra-entertaining gymnastic moves and special gestures that go along with the lyrics. Needless to say, the fans take it all in, and are soon following along. 'N Sync's live performances are definitely interactive. The fans, aside from singing along to every word in every song, hold up signs for the band to see when the house lights go on. The band likes to have a little fun with the audience, too, and has been known to squirt the crowd with water guns. The latest tour opened up with the five 'N Syncers in shiny space jumpsuits, their faces covered in white helmets as the strains of Darth Vader's *Star Wars* theme song filled the air. The band also incorporates cover versions of other artists' songs into its live show, including Kool and the Gang's hit "Celebration," "That Thing You Do" from the Tom Hanks movie, and even a Jackson Five medley.

'N Sync are pros at keeping their audience enthralled, and there is so much packed into their stage show it's no wonder fans travel from city to city to see them perform over and over again. The group wisely wants to keep their fans' attention every second, and surprises are the name of the game. As Lance says in the *'N the Mix* official home video, "When you look at us onstage, every song has a different feel to it." J.C. says he wants the fans to gasp, "Did you see that?" Fun and originality are important to this band. J.C. told *Faces in Pop* magazine, "We're all into what we do so much. We all love to sing, dance, write—do whatever we can to entertain. That's

what we share. This has never been about the fame or the money to us. It's always been about entertaining."

Aside from all of the rehearsing and planning that goes into their show, how do the boys prepare themselves for the adrenaline rush of running out onto the stage to the roar of the crowd each night? The band members de-stress and loosen up right before a show with a little help from their wardrobe assistants who double as licensed masseuses. That prepares them physically, but what about mentally? "We always pray before a show," Justin told *SuperTeen* magazine in its June 1999 issue. "We pray in the dressing room.

We get all the crew together and pray. . . . I say a prayer that we do a good show and we're safe. Then we get into a huddle and pump each other up before we go out on stage."

Any 'N Sync fan knows that the band is, without a doubt, five individual parts of a very highly tuned machine when it comes to their music. Believe it or not, they get along with the same syncopation behind the scenes. It's one-for-all and all-for-one. J.C. discussed the band's outlook during 'N Sync's April 24, 1998, American Online chat, stating, "Usually we agree but . . . if we don't, we talk it out and deal with it. Once we come to a decision on something, we all back it up completely."

The guys claim to get along like brothers, and that includes playing practical jokes on each other. A few standout pranks have been squeezing toothpaste into an unsuspecting band member's ear, or filling an empty tennis shoe with shaving cream. There has been at least one whipped-cream war, and a very tired Lance fell asleep in his dressing room once only to wake up covered in his Beanie Baby collection. On an airplane J.C. decided to take advantage of the down time and indulge in his favorite hobby—you guessed it, a little shut-eye—only to wake and discover Polaroids of himself sound asleep and covered in candy. Even the tubes of Rollos his prankster friends stuck in his ears didn't wake him up! "We're a family—just like any other perfectly dysfunctional family," J.C. laughingly told *Hit Sensation* magazine.

The band's tour bus is their home away from home. The guys chill out by watching movies on the road. Some of their favorites are *Austin Powers* and *Spinal Tap.* Joey's all-time favorite flick is *Willie Wonka and the Chocolate Factory.* What about rock 'n roll style misbehavior? Has 'N Sync ever been thrown out of a hotel for trashing the rooms or throwing television sets out the window like some rock stars? Of course not. As Joey disclosed during a Yahoo chat, "We've never been kicked out of one . . . but one time in London they told us that we couldn't come back because there were too many fans outside the hotel."

Even though the five 'N Syncers are extremely close, they still miss their friends and family back home. Justin told his fans on Yahoo that he is "very, very, very close" to his family, adding, "I miss them a lot on the road. I talk to my mother every day. I think I became closer to my family when I couldn't see them a lot. I never knew how much I valued family time until I didn't have it. I'm a family man." All of the guys are in close contact with home, sweet home, however—they would be lost without their cell-phones! Justin told *SuperTeen* magazine that the guys like to record silly messages on their phones, like, "Hi, I'm on stage right now, so as soon as I get done singing 'Tearin' Up My Heart' I'll call you back." The 'N Sync crew are all plugged in to the Internet as well. "I've got a computer that I use to go online at least once a week and say hello to all my friends. We always get in a chat room and I get to talk to like fifty of my friends at the same time, which is a lot easier on the cell bill," Lance told *Entertainment Weekly Online.* "And I go into 'N Sync chat rooms, and of course they never believe it's me." So, fans, keep on your toes!

Speaking of fans . . . 'N Sync have a very close relationship with their fans, and no matter how successful they are, they plan to keep it that way. Before every show they do a "Meet and Greet" with forty or fifty fans, just to get to know their audience. They consider it just as much a privilege to meet the people they will be performing for as the fans find it a thrill to meet their favorite artists in person.

Fans—especially girls!—will go to all lengths to meet 'N Sync. Sneaking into hotels, hiding under tables, and following the tour bus are frequent attempts, but the most daring was one smitten young lady who went for it suitcase-style, jumping on a baggage belt to get past airport security! As Britney Spears told the MTV Radio Network while she was touring with 'N Sync, "Oh my God, you should see these screaming girls. It's unreal. I mean, the things they do to see these guys is unbelievable."

'N Sync fans are nothing if not creative when it comes to showing their favorite band how devoted they are. Every day is Christmas for the 'N Sync five, as their fans bring gifts to every concert and send them presents in the mail. From Superman cakes and hand-knitted sweaters, poems, basketballs, and Beanie Babies to handcrafted miniatures of the band onstage and home videos of themselves lip-syncing to 'N Sync, the fans love to give something personal

back to thank the band for their great music. Of course the band can't keep all of the gifts they receive from their adoring fans—they would have a convoy of tour buses by now—so they donate all of the teddy bears, toys, and stuffed animals to children's hospitals.

The group has a lot of respect for their fans. "I think we really don't separate our fans into age groups, but I can tell you when it comes to littler kids we never talk down to them. . . . Kids are smart. We don't treat them like kids, we treat them like human beings," Chris revealed in his March 4, 1999, Yahoo chat session.

'N Sync fans do come in all ages, and some of them are as famous as the band members themselves. Kathy Griffin, the red-headed comedienne and co-star of Brooke Shields's hit TV series *Suddenly Susan*, has a running joke with the guys in 'N Sync, and tells everyone from MTV to Howard Stern that she is dating Joey. "Joey's 21, and he thinks I'm 28, and that's fine for everybody," she told *MTV News's* Chris Connelly. Joey's comeback, via MTV's John Norris, was to say that he and Kathy have been "married four years, have three kids, and live in Omaha, Nebraska." Fellow musical artist Ginuwine traveled to Florida just to meet 'N Sync and discuss recording a song or two together. "We kicked it off," he told MTV. "They're real cool guys, they're down to earth. Me and them were talking about duets and stuff like that and we spent about a week together. It was cool."

But back to the not-so-well-known ever-growing mass of loyal 'N Sync fans. A December 28, 1998, New York *Times* article entitled "The Roar of the Crowd" on the phenomena of screaming fans quoted an 'N Sync fan outside the MTV *Total Request Live* studios in New York City's Times Square. The fan, Karen La Plante, said, "I'm 18, so I'm not a teeny-bopper. I don't know what it is, but I just love 'N Sync. I've taken some pictures of Joey's arm, his head, Lansten's arm. All you see is yellow and red and blue, but it's worth it." Another, younger fan, fourteen-year-old Karen Lopez, was quoted as explaining, "Sometimes you say you're not going to scream, but then you do. . . . You're there, and then you start screaming, and then you scream some more. Your head hurts when you're finished, but you don't notice it while you're out here doing it." Well, J.C. may have put it best on the *'N Sync* enhanced CD when he said with a grin, "It's not exactly Beatlemania, but it's pretty cool."

So what is it about these five guys that drives their fans so crazy? We know their music is truly special, and their live shows are out of this world, but there is something about 'N Sync that you can't put your finger on . . . they try very hard to be accessible and grounded and, well, normal, but the fact remains that they have that superstar quality that is hard to come by.

The band's style is what J.C. dubs "conservative chaos." From Canadian designer Parasuco, Guess, and Fubu to Nike to Fila to DKNY to Adidas . . . Justin described the 'N Sync look to *SuperTeen* magazine as "pretty diverse. I think we can go from being very athletic to very dressed up. Some of us are a little more hip-hop and some of us are a little more dressy." When the band makes a bit of an effort to get formal and discards the sporty gear, their individual fashion senses come to light. J.C. favors tasteful leather jackets and, in keeping with his more conservative, classic hairstyle, rarely wears anything outrageous or too flashy (aside from the time the guys all dressed up as seventies groovers, complete with afro wigs, that is!). Lance is also a subtle dresser, leaning toward earth tones and forest greens, but there's one thing he always wears—his angelic smile. Justin goes for his all-time fave color, baby blue, even when he's wearing a suit, and pairs his outfits with color-coordinated sunglasses. Getting down to the wilder end of the spectrum, we find Joey, Jr., in bright reds, attention-grabbing accessories, and the infamous leopard-print overcoat he carried off with that mischievous grin of his. And the award for the all-out, over-the-top voguester of them all goes to Chris, hands down. His wild and unique hairstyle is just the icing on the cake for a guy who manages to pull together furry hats, gold lame, psychedelic swirls, patterned head-kerchiefs, and a touch of velvet to fab effect.

Of course, 'N Sync have developed their group image over the years. The original video for "I Want You Back" provides an interesting look at the band at the very beginning. The video, shot in a studio, features a younger-looking group of five guys—including a braidless Chris—who aren't as comfortable with themselves as the ultra-confident, free-spirited 'N Sync of today. Their dancing is less sophisticated and seems to lack the originality and spark of the group we all know and love. It seems the band realized this themselves, and when they set their sights on the U.S.A., they decided to reshoot the video to better represent what they had become. The U.S. video showcases the band's personality, showing the guys playing pool, basketball, and jet skiing. It has a bit of a story-line, as shots of J.C. driving the other four band members around, just cruising, are intermixed with shots of him dropping an angry girlfriend off at home.

The video for "Here We Go" has as its theme a game close to the

band's hearts: basketball. The on-court dance routine set in a high school gym is a lot of fun, and features a few of 'N Sync's signature pranks, including Lance hiding the ball under his shirt and Joey getting hit right on the head with it! "Here We Go" was slated to be the theme song for the NBA in 1998, but unfortunately due to the lockout it didn't come to be. Ah well, at least 'N Sync had their own basketball team, complete with red, white, and blue 'N Sync uniforms, at MTV's *Rock 'N Jock* in Malibu, California. Justin sported a gold 'N Sync necklace to complement his jersey. His team number? 1 1/2!

The "Tearin' Up My Heart" video made a permanent mark on the MTV airwaves, and really established the band as personalities. As Chris says in the *'N the Mix* official home video, "We don't consider ourselves anything but five guys doing what we love to do and having the time of our lives doing it, so with that we try to portray that as much as possible in the video." And that they did, with the photo-shoot premise of the video showing the guys at wardrobe and make-up, eating pizza, and just having fun. Of course, the slick performance side of things gets its time as well, and the segment featuring Justin singing on an iron bed clinched his heartthrob label for once and for all.

It was Chris's idea to set the "(God Must Have Spent) A Little More Time on You" video in the forties. The black and white video is really a mini-movie, and shows the love between a mother and son grow over the years, as the son grows up, falls in love, and goes to war. The surprise ending of the video is a great touch. 'N Sync shot the video at Blair High School in Pasadena, California, and during the shoot Joey realized that one of the female extras was actually a girl he knew from high school!

In the video for "The Girl Who Has Everything" the band enacts the song's story. The fivesome find themselves shipwrecked on a beautiful tropical island, and while they cavort in the waves, horseback ride on the beach, and play in waterfalls, the "Girl Who Has Everything" is miserably celebrating her birthday in her fabulous New York City home, being showered with expensive gifts that mean nothing to her. Finally, she wanders down to the river only to find the bottle the boys threw into the ocean, containing a photo of the guys inscribed with *"For the girl who has everything / I bring you love."*

Maybe it is the very fact that this hot group is made up of five very unique individuals that makes 'N Sync so intriguing and irresistible to their fans. Their very different personalities blend together so well to form such a strong bond, but it is their distinctive characters that spark so much interest above and beyond their music. To help fans answer the ultimate question, "Who's your favorite?" . . .

JUSTIN

Justin Randall Timberlake, born January 31, 1981, the baby of the group, is most often referred to as the band's number one heartthrob. Born in Memphis, Tennessee, he exhibited musical talent before he could even walk, keeping time to whatever music his parents would play. His father, Randy, was in a bluegrass band, and little Justin began harmonizing along almost before he could talk. Singing in church was a great joy to him. His first taste of pop star style performance came along when he was in the fourth grade and formed a New Kids on the Block lip-syncing act with some friends. At age eleven he performed a country song on *Star Search*, and it wasn't long before he landed a two-year-long spot on The *Mickey Mouse Club*. Of course, he had his mischievous side as a kid. As he admitted to *SuperTeen* in the magazine's June 1999 issue, "I was like Ferris Bueller. So if someone got in trouble, they always made sure they got in trouble with me, because I was in good with the teachers. I was a big negotiator."

The tallest member of the group, Justin, with his blue eyes and curly blonde hair, has natural good looks. However, he doesn't take his looks too seriously. He has dyed his hair almost every color of the rainbow, including red, blonde, green, and, of course, his favorite shade, baby blue. He's addicted to diamond earrings, sneakers, basketball (one of his idols is Michael Jordan), and cereal. Everyone knows not to speak to Justin until he's had his cereal–it's the only thing that wakes him up. Until he's downed a bowl of Oreos drowned in milk he's just sleepwalking! The kid in him is still alive and kicking: his favorite cartoon character is Bugs Bunny. Justin's fears are the three S's . . . spiders, snakes, and sharks, and his pet peeve is dishonesty. His hobbies include meditating, using his new lap-top, and writing songs and poetry.

Justin is a self-professed family man, and values the time he can spend with

his mom and stepdad and his father and stepmother. He absolutely adores his two stepbrothers. He spoke about his five-year-old brother, Jonathan, in *SuperTeen* magazine's June 1999 issue, saying, "It's so fun to watch him. I'll be sitting with my daddy and he's like, that's exactly how you were at that age. Jonathan can sing so well. He's got perfect pitch and he already hears harmonies and stuff." Jonathan reportedly goes to every 'N Sync concert he can! Steven, Justin's youngest brother, is only a baby and too young to realize that his big bro is a famous musical artist.

Okay, so let's get down to what every female 'N Sync fan who counts Justin as their fave really wants to know. What kind of person is he looking for in a girlfriend? "Confident, with a sense of humor, good listener, somebody with a sensitive heart," is how Justin described his perfect mate during his February 12, 1999, Yahoo chat. "I am a hopeless romantic, and I don't get off on people who make fun of other people. Somebody I could learn from, that would complement me, that could help me grow as a person." Justin's ideal girl is optimistic about life. He feels that there is too much pessimism in the world today. What about his first kiss? Justin admitted, "I was nervous. And I was with my girlfriend at that time. It was funny, now that I look back on how nervous I was. I wouldn't call it love, I would call it an infatuation. I think when you're in love with somebody you know it for sure." As unbelievable as it sounds to his fans, this heart-throb's only experience with real love (yet) was actually heartbreaking. He met her in 1995 at a party through mutual *MMC* buds. "Everything between us fitted in a minute! I was in love over both ears," Justin admitted to *Faces in Pop* magazine in its Winter Special '99 issue. "She ended it, she was secretly meeting with another boy. To me, it felt like my world collapsed—I was so hurt and sad! I had love pain for several months." Justin confesses to being a little gun-shy about falling head over heels again, although at this point in his life he's much too busy to fit a love affair into his schedule!

Joseph Anthony Fatone, Jr., was born (January 28, 1977) and raised in Brooklyn, New York, in a loving family. His father was a major influence on Joey Junior's desire to sing and perform; Joey's father sang in the Orions, a doo-wop group who performed all over New York and New Jersey. He was also very involved in the church and local theater, and would organize an annual Christmas show, which involved acting and music; needless to say, his son was happy to participate. Joey has been a ham ever since he was a toddler! Joey's early days were

filled with the sounds of the Temptations and Frankie Lymon and the Teenagers, as well as more contemporary groups like Boyz II Men. The stylish Joey of today attended a Catholic school called St. Mary's as a kid, and had to wear a uniform and tie every day.

When Joey had just turned a teenager, he, his parents, and his sister Janine and brother Steven moved to Orlando, Florida. When Joey first went to Florida, his father tricked him into it! Joe Fatone, Sr., told his kids that he was going on a business trip, and suggested that they come with him to the airport to see the inside of an airplane for the first time. It wasn't until the captain announced that it was time to fasten seatbelts in preparation for take-off that Joey's parents told their children that in fact they were all off to sunny Florida! The kids had fallen lock, stock, and barrel for the prank—they didn't even realize that their parents had packed suitcases for them!

It was in Orlando that Joey began to seriously develop his acting, dancing, and singing talent. He acted in *Matinee* and *SeaQuest*, but his favorite acting stint to date was his small part in the film *Once upon a Time in America*. He told *Celebrity Series Presents* magazine, "I was honored to play that role simply because the story was fantastic and I got to act in the same film as my idol Robert DeNiro." As luck would have it, he landed a gig at Universal Studios after high school—and we all know where that led.

Nowadays Joey's full-time job is performing, but his hobbies have remained the same. As any 'N Sync fan knows, Joey is crazy about Superman and collects any memorabilia he can get his hands on. He may wear Superman shirts and a Superman necklace today, but as a kid he wore a cape—and even tried to fly, which earned him more than a few scrapes and bruises. He loves going clubbing, going to the movies, and just hanging out with his friends. His favorite food? Italian, of course. Joey also gets a thrill out of traveling, and when on the road with 'N Sync he discovered that he loved South Africa and Asia, and was very impressed with Germany's architecture.

What about girls? Joey is known as the flirt of the group, but he made a surprising confession during his December 10, 1998, Yahoo chat. He claimed, "I got dumped on my first date! I took her to the movies. And she dumped me!" He added with his typical good humor, "I guess the movie wasn't that good." Joey has a great sense of humor—you can tell by his smile—and doesn't take anything too seriously. He doesn't mind making fun of himself. When *Tiger Beat* magazine asked Joey about his favorite body part, he said, "The worst is my feet—because I step on everything. Best? My nose, because it's big and I can smell a lot of food." When asked on Yahoo what one thing he couldn't do without, Joey jokingly replied, "Clothes. I wouldn't want to run around naked." Most importantly, Joey knows it is important to remain grounded despite 'N Sync's overwhelming success. Joey confessed in his March 11, 1999, Yahoo chat that he can't let fame go to his head, saying, "All of us keep each other on the ground and if I had a chip on my shoulder or a big head about this . . . my mom would kick my butt!"

It is difficult for fans of the confident, heartfelt singer J.C. (Joshua Scott Chasez, born in Washington, D.C., on August 8, 1976) to believe that he grew up a very shy guy. It was only his love of the dancing styles of M.C. Hammer and Bell Biv Devoe that really got him into all of this. He was dared by some female friends to enter a dance competition with them, and lo and behold, they won! He soon recovered from his bashfulness, and got up the courage to sing–and could he ever sing. His very first audition for anything was for the *Mickey Mouse Club*, and he was one of ten kids chosen from 20,000 who gave it a shot, and was on the show for four fulfilling years.

It seems that J.C. was just biding his time as a kid, enjoying a normal family life with his parents, sister Heather, and brother Tyler. Some of his favorite memories are very adventurous family vacations. He told *SuperTeen* magazine, "We always went and did wild and weird road trips. We were like the Griswalds from *National Lampoon's Family Vacation* . . . we would drive anywhere . . . we've seen freak shows on Route 66, we've seen it all." J.C. wanted to be a carpenter or an architect or an antique car restorer when he was younger, but 'N Sync fans are thankful that none of those career choices worked out.

His hobbies today include collecting Hard Rock Café menus, and he wears a lion necklace in honor of his star sign, Leo. He loves all of the Star Wars movies; in fact, his first crush was Star Wars' Princess Leia! Restless J.C. brings a yo-yo on tour with him. As Justin told *Faces in Pop* magazine, "J.C.'s always moving–he has to be dancing around or doing something in the background." Despite all of his energy, the band call him Sleepy Spice; he's the first to admit that 'N Sync's grueling schedule doesn't give him much time for one of his favorite pastimes–a little shut-eye.

J.C.'s sculpted cheekbones and soulful eyes are enough to make any girl sigh. However, the good-looking J.C. is attracted to someone who is secure with themselves, and not hung up on how they look. He described his ideal date on Yahoo, saying it would have to be "somewhere quiet. So I can get to know that person. I don't need a lot of noise and hype and all that. I want to be able to chat and get to know each other."

First and foremost, J.C. is a perfectionist, and a true professional. He sticks to his principles no matter what. "I wouldn't go on TV grabbing this, that, or the other and have my parents looking at that," J.C. told *People Online* in its February 8, 1999, issue. "That's just the way I was raised." He's also been called Serious Spice, and the fact that he takes his role as a pop star and entertainer very seriously indeed is one key to his success.

CHRIS

Christopher Alan Kirkpatrick, the oldest member of 'N Sync—and the one who came up with the fantastic idea of the band in the first place—was born in Clarion, Pennsylvania, on October 17, 1971. He comes from a very, very musical family. Both sets of his great-grandparents were in bands; his grandmother was an opera singer; his grandfather was a country and western singer who recorded five albums; his aunts and uncles are in bands from country, rock, and jazz to rockabilly; and his mother teaches voice lessons and plays several instruments. How's that for having music in the blood?

Chris was always getting himself into something as a kid—it looks like things haven't changed. He has a scar over his left eye, which he got while misbehaving as a youngster; he was chasing his sister and hit a wall. "I was a serious kid," Chris jokingly told *SuperTeen* magazine in its May 1999 issue. "No, I was a trouble-maker! I was rambunctious. I was real hyper. But I was always into music. I loved music. I've got pictures, I've got little films of me singing, doing Oliver Twist, doing all these little musicals." In high school Chris had lead roles in many school plays. He graduated from Orlando's Valencia Community College in 1993, the same school Backstreet Boy Howie Dorough attended. Although Chris loves the music industry, and always had it in his mind to pursue a career as a performer, he seriously considered becoming a psychologist, and majored in psychology in addition to his theater and music classes.

Chris is definitely the craziest member of 'N Sync. In keeping with his reputation, he even goofed on the typist helping him out during his Yahoo chat by stating that his New Year's Resolution was "To stop saying supercalifragilisticexpialidocious." When another fan asked him if he believed in aliens, claiming to be the victim of an abduction, Chris replied, "Hmmm . . . So was I . . . Let's go seek counseling together" and was quick to come up with being "force fed cooked carrots" as his least favorite activity. He then jokingly described his method for escaping fan attention, saying, "I can't really disguise myself. I dress up as Justin sometimes—that seems to work." When asked who would play him in a movie, Chris comes up with Bette Midler. He loves tacos, and has named himself Refried Bean Spice.

The story of Chris's first kiss came out online, during his Yahoo chat. Even when it comes to love, Chris can't help but joke around. He claimed, "It was awkward b/c we were playing Kiss Tag so after she kissed me she punched me. So had to learn at a very young age that women are nothing but trouble ;-)."

The guy with the wild hairstyle and endless energy loves children and takes his role as a performer very seriously indeed. His psychology studies helped him learn about music therapy and how good music is for the soul; he knows the power of music. He loves to chill out in his spare time (if he ever has any) and spin records on his turntable. He carries a small Indian shield and a cross with him for good luck. Chris told 'N Sync fans on Yahoo, "I'd love to be a tree, because trees just seem so knowledgeable and such a permanent thing on earth."

Chris may be known as a jokester, always handy with a quick comeback or a witty answer, but he remains, underneath it all, very serious about what matters. When asked by *Celebrity Series Presents* about fame, he replied, "Being famous means changing and we don't want that to happen. It is our job to stay grounded and not to change our personalities." He went on to say, "Our aim is to be good, as good as we can be, but we also have to be individuals."

The mellow, calm, and relaxed Lance wasn't always that way. It seems that James Lance Bass, born on May 4, 1979, in Clinton, Mississippi, was quite a handful! He confessed to *SuperTeen* magazine that he "was like a really crazy idiot when I was little. I was very hyper; that's all I loved to do was just play and play. I was just a little comedian —everyone was like, 'You're gonna grow up to be a comedian.' And then I really matured and now I'm laid back. I totally changed." It must be in honor of his earlier manic days that Lance's pet mascot today is the Tasmanian Devil.

It has been reported that Lance came close to his original career dream of becoming an astronaut by passing the NASA entrance examination! We do know that he attended Space Camp at Camp Kennedy when he was in the seventh grade. He told *SuperTeen* magazine that the experience "was so much fun. After that, I was just like, that's what I want to do. We had to simulate shuttle missions and all that kind of stuff. It was incredible. I loved the whole thing." Lance used to work at a daycare center in Mississippi until he received that fateful phone call from Justin's vocal coach. He played baseball, football, and basketball at school, and his favorite subjects were science and math. He still keeps at his academics, taking courses through the University of Nebraska. Lance collects Beanie Babies, plays keyboards, and reads the Bible in his spare time. He is a water person, and loves jet skiing and water-skiing.

Green-eyed Lance is looking for a girl with whom he could be close friends first, with the hope that the relationship would blossom over time into something more. He revealed during his Yahoo chat what his ideal female companion would be, saying, "I like the innocent type. The good girls. I like a religious girl. Someone I can talk to and be best friends with for anything."

He truly seems to relish the opportunity to see the world; as he says in the *'N the Mix* official home video, "Being on tour is one of the highlights of being in this business—getting to travel all over the world, getting to see city after city, meet new people . . . it's an incredible feeling." Lance loved Liechtenstein "because it's the most peaceful country you'll probably ever go to," he reminisced during his Yahoo chat session, calling it "just paradise." Most people go to tropical islands in order to relax, but not Lance. During his trip to Cancun he ended up in a bullfight! And he will be the first to tell you that it was an extremely painful and frightening experience. Maybe next time he'll just soak up the sun and read a good book.

Lance's nickname, Scoop, was given to him by Joey's brother Steve, who relies on Lance to keep him up-to-date on the band's activities as Lance always memorizes the 'N Sync itinerary. And it's no secret

that Lance has a head for business, and is extremely interested in all of the behind-the-scenes music industry operations behind the creation and maintenance of a successful band like 'N Sync. Joey described Lance in *Teen Dream* magazine's April 1999, issue, saying, "He's such a good person to talk to. He's really knowledgeable about business and marketing and is always on top of things." Here's just one example: Lance, the future industry executive, showed his head for business when it came to the band's next single. RCA had "For the Girl Who Has Everything" slated as the next hit, but Lance mentioned that he felt that most fans' favorite was "(God Must Have Spent) A Little More Time on You" and that he thought it would be wise to switch choices. The record company took Lance's suggestion seriously enough to launch an online contest in which fans could vote on the band's next single—and guess which song came out way on top! Maybe next time they'll pay heed to Lance's hunches!

'N Sync has certainly come a long way from their humble beginnings as five young guys with a dream and a lot of determination. The days when Joey's mother, Phyllis, stored the band's fan mail in her living room are long gone. Proof positive that 'N Sync's popularity has reached just about every corner of the world came on May 2, 1999, when the Caribbean islands of St. Vincent and the Grenadines issued an official 'N Sync postage stamp. The Postmaster of St. Vincent told *MTV News* on April 28, 1999, that she felt 'N Sync were fit for stampdom as the band "represented the best of what art and entertainment can present to young people, as they are positive role models with a positive message." Quite an honor. Even Elvis had to wait until he had entered the Kingdom Come before his stamp came to be!

It seemed that every move 'N Sync made was big news. Even a little thing like a stray water balloon made headlines when the band's autograph signing session at the Mall of America in Bloomington, Minnesota, was cut short. An unidentified assailant (a jealous male teenager perhaps?) shattered thousands of girl teens dreams—many of whom had been camping out outside of the shopping mall since 3:00 A.M. —of meeting the band by dropping a water balloon on the unsuspecting throng from the shopping mall's balcony. "People were throwing stuffed animals and stink bombs, and a water balloon hit a couple of fans," Lance told the Minneapolis *Star Tribune* in its May 7, 1999, edition. "So for the protection of the fans, security felt it was best to end it."

The Spring 1999 tour barreled along, coming to a triumphant close with no less than five shows in the guys' old stomping ground of Florida. Lance missed out on the homecoming fun, however, as he became very ill and spent a few nights in the hospital while the other four were on stage. Reports that he was suffering from a stomach virus or had collapsed from exhaustion abounded, although Lance himself brushed his illness off during his September 1, 1999, Yahoo! chat, saying, "I have a slight heart condition, but it's nothing to worry about."

The guys then went straight into the studio to record their next album, which they planned to release in November. Little did they know that there was trouble ahead, and the album would be delayed until March, 2000. Just to be sure that they wouldn't go into withdrawal from the rush of onstage performance, the fivesome joined B*Witched and U.K. pop sensation Billie at the opening ceremony of the Women's World Cup on June 19 at New Jersey's Giants Stadium.

A starstruck 'N Sync's earlier collaboration in 1999 with Phil Collins for the soundtrack to Disney's *Tarzan* movie paved the way for more musical partnerships. Although the 'N Syncers may feel like pinching themselves while working with some of music's biggest names, it's often a strange experience for the seasoned pros themselves. "I felt a little bit like their dad, to be honest," Phil Collins told *Entertainment Weekly Online* on June 4, 1999. "I felt a little awkward until Chris said to me, 'You know, this is very strange for me. The first record I bought was *No Jacket Required*, and here I am singing with you.' And suddenly I felt… well, I still felt like his dad, but I felt okay." He was very happy with 'N Sync's professionalism, however, telling *People Online*, "I was pleased with them because in addition to being so popular they're also good singers, and some of these groups aren't such good singers."

With a little help from some cowboy-hatted friends, 'N Sync went country with the June 1999 release of Alabama's album *20th Century*. The album featured the country greats' cover version of 'N Sync's own "(God Must Have Spent) A Little More Time on You," featuring Chris, J.C., Joey, Justin, and Lance on backing vocals. The band couldn't believe it when Alabama contacted them about recording it; clairvoyant Lance had declared that the tune would make a perfect country song from day one! The band hit the stage at the Grand Ole Opry House on September 22 to perform the song with Alabama for the Thirty-third Annual Country Music Awards.

It seemed that melodious unions with other artists were yet another of 'N Sync's fortes, and their next Number One hit single confirmed it. The band recorded the beautiful ballad "Music of My Heart" with Gloria Estefan for the *Music of the Heart* soundtrack. The film, whose theme is the importance of music education, stars Gloria Estefan in her film debut along with award-winning actress Meryl Streep. The 'N Sync five admitted to being starstruck yet again while filming the video for the single, which was directed by Nigel Dick, who has also worked on Britney Spears and Ricky Martin videos. The song would prove to have staying power, and was to be nominated for an Oscar; Gloria and the boys performed a quick version of the Oscar-nominated song at the Academy Awards 2000.

Both musical partnerships earned accolades at the Forty-second Annual Grammy Awards Show on February 23, 2000. 'N Sync were presenters at the ceremony, but they were also two-time nominees, with "Music of My Heart" up for Best Pop Collaboration with Vocals and "(God Must Have Spent) A Little More Time on You" up for Best Country Collaboration with Vocals.

Just a few days after the Fourth of July fireworks, the band's big summer tour began with a resounding bang on July 7 at the Virginia Beach Amphitheatre. Night after night of sold out stadium shows filled the hot summer nights with the sound of screaming girls as 'N Sync made its way across the country. In many cities, the band played multiple nights and still couldn't satisfy every would-be ticket-holder. The three-month-long tour stopped off in New Jersey, Pennsylvania, New York, Massachusetts, Connecticut, Ohio, Michigan, Indiana, Tennessee, Missouri, Illinois, Wisconsin, Kansas, Louisiana, Texas, Arizona, California, Colorado, Georgia, North Carolina, and Mississippi before finally reaching its grand finale in Canada.

A schedule like this would exhaust most ordinary humans, but 'N Sync even managed to squeeze in more studio time here and there during the tour. They knew that their next album was their chance to prove that they had staying power, and they were dedicated and determined to make it the best they could. In fact, the five California and Las Vegas dates were rescheduled for the end of November so that the band could put the final touches on their new album in the studio in time for its November 16 release date. Fans were very understanding—particularly as the shows were just delayed, not canceled.

The five guys absolutely love to perform, and as they would be the first to tell you, every show was special to them. Of course, the gig in Hershey Park had its roller coaster and chocolate bonus. The band's New Orleans show was one to remember, as Lance invited a couple of hundred of his closest friends to the concert. They all sat in the first few rows and teased and taunted their famous 'N Sync friends mercilessly throughout the show. Rumor has it that J.C. almost missed a verse due to laughing! Aside from presents and flowers, fans sometimes shower their favorite band with—believe it or not—underwear. As Lance recalled during his September 1, 1999, Yahoo! chat, "One time Joey picked up a bra and put it on our drummer's head as he was playing. That was pretty funny."

The last show of each tour is certain to be a memorable one, and the Canadian show was no exception. The band had their entire crew on stage to thank them for all of their hard work, leading the crowd in a chant of "'N Sync Crew! 'N Sync Crew!" Not every fan realizes how much behind-the-scenes work goes into the fantastic show the band puts on. The elaborate 'N Sync stage show—and most of the crew—is loaded up into no less than eight semis and trucked overnight to the next venue after every show. Well, the band's gracious thank-you was returned with a bit of revenge… when the boys flew back to the stage after squirting the audience with their water pistols, they were left hanging in midair, defenseless, as their devoted crew came onstage once again, this time to give them a good soaking!

Luckily, the 'N Sync five can take a joke. In fact, the band is not known to take itself too seriously, a fate that often befalls successful groups. David Letterman may have created his own mock boy band, Fresh Step, but 'N Sync parodied their own genre during a *Saturday Night Live* skit called "Seven Degrees Celsius." The band is also not afraid of self-criticism. As Jason reflected in *Rolling Stone's* March 30, 2000, cover story, the 'N Sync live show "might be better if it wasn't such a spectacle. Maybe people would respect it more."

Local concert reviews, although all a bit skeptical at the outset, had to admit that there was justification for all that screaming. "'N Sync's performance was a vivid demonstration of the ever-evolving multimedia events concerts have become," wrote Tom Maurstad of the Dallas *Morning News*. "The fab five from Florida delivered a spectacular song-and-dance revue filled with action, drama, romance… and comedy. These guys were a veritable entertainment machine," said Mike Ross of the Edmonton *Sun*. The Minneapolis *Star Tribune's* Jon Bream wrote, "What makes the music work onstage is the impressive vocal harmonies and the energetic, entertaining presentation."

It seemed that everyone agreed that the summer tour was a rousing success. Each show began with up to five support acts, and that was just the appetizer. The suspense mounted, but wait—just as Chris, J.C., Joey, Justin, and Lance were due to hit the stage and the volume level of the crowd's screams was reaching all-new heights—a stern face appeared on a huge screen to notify the audience that he had sealed off the doors, blocking the band's entrance! The evil man had put a stop to "that dreadful noise you call fun music." But never fear, faithful fans. Helicopter sound effects roared, communications from the band via walkie-talkies assured, and sparks flew as the band members broke through the stadium roof with the help of welding torches. Taking the stage by sliding down ropes from high above to the *Mission Impossible* theme was an 'N Sync-style stunt that set the mood for an evening packed with entertainment. The band kept up the sixties, seventies, and eighties musical-revue segment of their show complete with Beatles and Jackson Five getups. A few lucky girls were brought on stage every night to be personally serenaded during the band's performance of "The Girl Who Has Everything." Thoughtful as ever, the guys ensured that each and every fan enjoyed the show as giant video screens offered up front-seat views to the furthest reaches of the stadiums. In fact, they even *visited* the cheap seats while flying overhead during their rendition of "Sailing," touching hands with the ecstatic audience.

Any 'N Sync fan knows that the guys love to help out with charities whenever they have the chance. The five pop stars also love sports, and they warmed up for their August 8 show in Milwaukee by playing a little softball. The band and some of their crew took on a local team in front of 3,000 fans who all brought canned goods to donate to food banks; the ticket proceeds also went to help feed the homeless. Later that month the band sponsored the "Challenge for Children" charity basketball event in Atlanta on August 25 which featured the hoop skills of fellow musical personalities Jermaine Dupri, Jordan Knight, Mase, Busta Rhymes, Usher, and members of Outkast and Blackstreet as well as some bona fide NBA players. The event raised funds to support local charities and hospitals, as well as relief efforts for the devastating earthquake in Turkey. "It's just so good that we can have this much fun and then have a turnout like this," Justin told *MTV News* after the game. "So many charities benefit from it. When we originally had this idea, we didn't know it would go this far, and we're very proud that everyone came out."

Although the guys have a packed-out schedule year-round, they always make it a priority to make time to raise money and awareness for good causes. And anyway, who says doing good can't be good fun? The 'N Sync five had a blast laying down the track "Love's in Our Hearts on Christmas Day" for Rosie O'Donnell's duet-fueled Christmas CD, *A Rosie Christmas*, which featured the likes of Celine Dion, Billy Joel, Gloria Estefan, Elton John, Cher, Lauryn Hill, and more. Rosie and all of the artists donated the album's proceeds to the O'Donnell-founded nonprofit For All Kids Foundation.

In August the band joined up with Britney Spears, Christina Aguilera, LFO, and 98 Degrees for the UPN televised concert called *L'Oreal Paris Summer Music Mania '99*. All of the performers donated a percentage of their fee to the A Friend of Mine Foundation, set up to aid survivors of the Columbine High School shooting.

VH1's *Concert of the Century*, a star-studded show on the South Lawn of the White House, had as its admirable goal the promotion of the significance of music education in the nation's school systems. The October 1999 concert raised funds for VH1's Save the Music Foundation. 'N Sync and Gloria Estefan performed "Music of My Heart"; other celebrity performers and speakers included Eric Clapton, Gwyneth Paltrow, Sheryl Crow, Lenny Kravitz, Calista Flockhart, B.B. King, John Mellencamp, Robert de Niro, and Garth Brooks.

'N Sync took the stage along with Destiny's Child, Joey McIntyre, Monica, and Wyclef Jean at New York City's Beacon Theater for LIFEbeat's twelfth annual World AIDS Day concert on December 1. The focus of the show was the "Zero Transmission 2001" drive which aims at education and HIV and AIDS prevention amongst teens. Lance told *MTV News*, "It's a very important issue for us. Hopefully if we all got together, we can find a cure someday." It was a busy day, even in the ultramanic world of 'N Sync, as the band also made an appearance at the city's Sixty-seventh annual Rockefeller Center tree-lighting ceremony along with fellow performers Britney Spears and Enrique Iglesias. As any 'N Sync fan knows, the guys love Christmas, and they also couldn't resist joining the Yuletide march for the Walt Disney World Very Merry Christmas Parade along with Harry Connick, Jr., and 98 Degrees.

The band also participated in Nickelodeon's December 11 "Big Holiday Help-a-thon," joining the ranks of Britney Spears, Aaron Carter, and Big Help spokespeople Elton John and Mariah Carey in the effort to encourage young people to take on volunteer work.

'N Sync's charity connection took a strange turn in March 2000 when a piece of French toast earned the band's charity of choice a tasty $2,050. It all began with breakfast (as every day should) at New York City's Z100 radio station. The band showed up to have a little *petit dejuener* with contest winners, and the entrepreneurial staff, upon discovering that one of the band members had left his French toast virtually untouched, decided to offer the tidbit to the highest bidder on the online auction house eBay. A female college student in Wisconsin shelled out $1,025 for the surely soggy lump of bread, and Z100 matched her bid. All the fuss back in the Beatlemania days over crazed Beatles fans trading cold hard cash for squares of sheets the Fab Four had slept in somehow pales in comparison.

Anyone who knows the 'N Sync five knows that it is impossible for them to sit still. Just two days after the final show of the summer tour, the guys took to the stage again—this time at the September 9 MTV Video Music Awards at New York City's Metropolitan Opera House. They teamed up with Britney Spears on a schoolroom set for her performance of "…Baby One More Time" during which 'N Sync members masqueraded as students sitting dutifully at their desks. They then revealed their true identities and launched into "Tearin' Up My Heart" which was nominated for Best Pop Video, Best Group Video, and the Viewer's Choice Award.

Die-hard fans also had another opportunity to catch a glimpse of their favorite five on television in September with the band's Pay-Per-View special, *'N Sync 'N Concert*, which was a chance for everyone who hadn't been lucky enough to score concert tickets to experience the live show. The group also debuted their newest video, "You Drive Me Crazy," with its insane-asylum/straitjacket theme. In the generous spirit of 'N Sync, the first half-hour preview of the pay event was free of charge.

Then came the stunning announcement that would put the future of 'N Sync in jeopardy: the band was leaving BMG's RCA Records and moving to Jive Records. Johnny Wright revealed plans to delay the release of the new album rather than rushing to put it out. Jive, home of both Britney Spears and the Backstreet Boys, was thrilled. RCA was not. Nor, allegedly, were the Backstreet Boys whose deal reportedly had to be yet again renegotiated to the tune of $60 million and a 20% royalty rate to smooth things over.

An ominous statement, which read, "'N Sync is a BMG act and we enforce and protect our rights vigorously" was RCA's response. Then there was silence—the lull before the storm—during which time lawyers gathered their ammunition. It wasn't long, however, before the scorned label unleashed its fury in the form of $150 million dollar lawsuit. BMG Entertainment, along with Louis Pearlman, Trans Continental Media, and Trans Continental Records, filed the suit against 'N Sync, Jive Records, and its parent company Zomba in Federal Court in Orlando, Florida, in October for breach of management and recording contracts. *MTV News* issued the disturbing report that Pearlman's attorneys told MTV that the lawsuit "seeks to obtain a court order to prevent 'N Sync from existing." VH1 reported that "J. Cheney Mason, a counsel for Trans Continental, described the injunction at the time as part of their legal 'scorched-earth policy. We're going to shut them down. We believe there will be no tours, no performances, no rehearsal or recordings.'"

Mud slinging in the disguise of prepared statements commenced. "We hope everyone will do the right thing so the group can be where it belongs, which is onstage, rather than in a court of law," went BMG's statement. "It is absurd to think that now that the members of 'N Sync have been made rich and famous, they can just turn their backs on Mr. Pearlman and Trans Continental and go someplace else," protested Michael D. Friedman, a lawyer representing Pearlman and Trans Continental, in his statement.

What a mess! 'N Sync issued a statement with the bombshell comment that "Trans Continental's conduct with regard to 'N Sync is the most glaring, overt, and callous example of artist exploitation that the music industry has seen in a long time." Wow—tell us how you *really* feel! Lou "Big Papa" Pearlman, who had been credited with fostering the group and putting them on the map insisted that the band's statement wasn't really how the band felt, and certainly wasn't about him. He explained to *MTV News* on October 27 that it just wasn't like that, making the surprising claim that it was all much ado about nothing. He maintained that Trans Con had no choice but to join BMG in legal action, saying, "It's not us wanting to sue the boys, and that's the last thing that we would ever want to do, is sue them. I think it blew out of proportion, because the paperwork looks like we are, but we're still as friendly as can be, and it's a tight family, and we'll stay that way."

However it seemed that "the boys" weren't feeling quite as friendly and begged to differ. The band filed a $25 million countersuit against Pearlman and Trans Continental—not BMG. 'N Sync described Pearlman as "an unscrupulous, greedy, and sophisticated businessman who posed as an unselfish, loving father figure and took advantage of our trust" in their counterclaim (the band's written response to the lawsuit against them which included statements from Johnny Wright and Lance and Justin's mothers). J.C.'s statement was perhaps the most shocking, saying that Pearlman, "while hugging us and calling us 'family', was picking our pockets, robbing us of our future, and even endangering our health."

The band's ever-loyal fans followed the legal wranglings carefully. They organized protests and rallies and even conceived a petition urging United States Congress to pass a prohibitive ruling so that future young pop stars would not be unfairly treated.

The lawsuit was complicated as well as quite unprecedented. 'N Sync's claim was that their April 1996 agreement with Pearlman and Trans Con was totally unfair to the band in that Pearlman was pocketing a staggeringly disproportionate percentage of the band's earnings. (Some reports claimed that Pearlman allotted himself up to two-thirds of all merchandising and record royalties and 100 percent of the publishing.) The band also claimed that Pearlman had never actually secured them an American record deal, as RCA was simply licensing 'N Sync's records from its German label, Ariola. Yet another complication was the fact that BMG was Jive's North American distributor and actually a twenty percent owner of Zomba. Despite the various factors, the focus of the case soon became Louis Pearlman, who for once wasn't enjoying the spotlight.

As a matter of fact, it was reported in *USA Today's* November 22, 1999, edition that Pearlman was entertaining the idea of selling Trans Continental. "We are looking to have another company acquire us to give us more working capital," he told the newspaper. Interesting timing.

One music industry attorney, Jill Berliner—who did not even represent 'N Sync—went as far as to file papers in court as an expert witness to help argue their case, stating that 'N Sync's deals with Trans Continental were "classic contracts of adhesion imposed upon an uncounseled and unskilled, highly susceptible group of teenagers." Berliner was further quoted in *Rolling Stone's* December 29, 1999, issue as commenting that "the overview, the combination of documents, is just breathtaking in its aggressiveness."

Michael D. Friedman, Pearlman's lawyer, was quoted in *Teen People's* February 11, 2000, edition as asserting that "without Lou, there would be no 'N Sync. These five young men might well be among the thousands of talented young performers who took a shot at the highly competitive music business and remain in obscurity." Pearlman was quoted in *Rolling Stone's* December 29, 1999, issue as having said, "I paid the bills. I gave them a house; I paid their living expenses, for vocal coaches, choreography. I didn't hear anybody talking back then that [the deals] weren't fair. For the next three years they weren't unfair. I was out three million dollars…I mean gimme a break."

Judge Anne Conway was not inclined to give Pearlman a break. On the day before Thanksgiving a court hearing took place at which the Trans Continental team attempted to convince the judge to rule that 'N Sync could not move to Jive Records until a trial took place, which might be as far off as 2002. Judge Conway, however, far too intrigued as to how much money Pearlman had made through his relationship with 'N Sync, ruled that the band could indeed move ahead with their Jive deal, and advised the opposing sides to come to an agreement through mediation rather than going to trial.

And, to the collective relief of 'N Sync fans around the world, the warring factions did indeed reach a settlement, just days before Christmas. The 'N Sync crew was free to begin the new year with Jive Records and without the stress and worry of legal battles. The final word came in the form of a statement from 'N Sync, BMG Entertainment, Trans Continental, and the Zomba Group as posted on the band's web site, which read, "Thanks to the efforts of everyone involved in recent negotiations, multi-platinum group 'N Sync and the Zomba Group have settled out of court with BMG Entertainment, Louis Pearlman, and Pearlman's Trans Continental Group. All parties involved are extremely pleased with the speedy resolution of this matter. 'N Sync will be able to build on the international success they have enjoyed with BMG and Trans Continental through a new worldwide recording contract with the Zomba Group's Jive Records. Although specifics of the settlement cannot be disclosed, 'N Sync will enjoy the right to control their name. In addition, the Zomba Group has extended its distribution agreement with BMG for North America. 'N Sync, Zomba, BMG, and Trans Continental look forward to benefiting from the future success of 'N Sync. There will be no further comment regarding this settlement."

NO STRINGS

Free to pursue their musical dreams without the threat of lawsuits, the loss of their collective name, or any other creative restraints, 'N Sync was determined to start the new century on their own terms. A decidedly footloose and fancy-free 'N Sync bid farewell to their troubles and debuted their brand-new single, aptly titled "Bye Bye Bye," at the American Music Awards on January 17, 2000. The song's video, which features the boys running away from (yes, that's right, *away* from) gorgeous seventeen-year-old model Kim Smith, was a tantalizing peak at the new attitude of the much anticipated *No Strings Attached*. The band, although a little older and a little wiser, still knows how to have fun, and the James Bond style video includes a car chase, a Doberman pinscher chase, a girl-chase, and an on-top-of-a-train chase. The video is as stylish as it is energetic. The 'N Sync five developed the plot of the video themselves, from its opening showing the puppet-on-a-string fivesome being cut loose. "We just want a fast paced video," J.C. told MTV during the filming of the video, directed by Wayne Isham, who has worked with both Backstreet Boys and Ricky Martin as well as Mötley Crüe and Metallica. "We came up with a concept—the song is a love song, but it's about kissing somebody off. They burned you and now they want you back and you're like, 'Sorry.'"

Lest we forget, in the midst of recording their all-important sophomore album, the boys found themselves, in effect, without a record label. Although many bands would have panicked, 'N Sync actually seemed to enjoy the freedom this unusual situation afforded them, and found that they could employ whom they wanted to work with, without bigwig label heads putting constraints on the process. As Lance told Roger Coletti of the MTV Radio Network on January 26, at some points the band was "totally independent, and so we had to independently do the album. We had to pay for it. We had to go out there and search for songs, write songs, and record in a little bitty studio at our manager's place."

So how would *No Strings Attached* fare? Would it be worth the wait? Would it prove that 'N Sync was a true talent to be reckoned with, one that would outlast and outgrow the "boy band" stigma? Would it—could it—break the sales record set by Backstreet Boys last album? "I doubt it," Jeff Pollack, a top radio consultant, told the Los Angeles *Times* in its March 17, 2000, edition. "It will be a huge record, but being bigger than *Millennium*—that's asking a lot." Jive President Barry Weiss was optimistic in *Billboard's* March 20 "Hot Product" section, saying, "The public has been waiting with bated breath. The fact that the drama played out in the public forum only heightened awareness of the new album. Fans are crying for it."

The much-delayed release date of *No Strings Attached* finally arrived on March 21, 2000. And what a day! Jive Records shipped a staggering 4.2 million copies of the album out to stores. The label's own vice president of national sales, Bob Anderson, was quoted on *Sonicnet* as saying, "This is really an unprecedented number for us—it's a giant initial shipment." Virgin and Tower record stores across the country stayed open past 12AM on March 20 in order to sell the album at the stroke of midnight. In an article entitled "'N Sync on Historic Pace," *Billboard* reported on March 23 that "with first-day sales believed to be about 950,000 units from the top fifteen retail and racked accounts alone, 'N Sync's Jive debut *No Strings Attached* is already challenging the SoundScan one-week sales record of 1.13 million units set by Backstreet Boys' *Millennium*. The album is expected to debut at No. 1 on The Billboard 200 next week."

And what of the accusations that 'N Sync is riding on the tails of the Backstreet Boys's success? "Jimmy crack corn, and I don't care," Joey told the Los Angeles *Times* in its March 17, 2000, issue. "I don't have a reaction to the references. If the people that made that statement hear this new album, they will know what they said was false…When you run the race, you don't look behind you, you look forward." More than just a positive attitude, Joey's words proved themselves to be true when *No Strings Attached* confirmed 'N Sync's very own place in pop music history.

The band created absolute mayhem in New York City's Times Square as thousands of fans crowded the streets to peek up at the plate-glass windows of MTV's *Total Request Live* studios. How the fearless five managed to cross Broadway to the neighboring Virgin Megastore for an autograph session is anyone's guess—maybe all that practice flying in concert paid off—but they did, satisfying the 500 fans who had passes, some of whom had been patiently waiting since the weekend. The five pop stars were forced to take precautions in the form of motorcades and members of the NYPD in riot gear. Even unflappable, blasé, been-there-seen-that New York paid a bit of attention to all the fuss. The evening news stations reported on the spectacle with enthusiasm usually reserved for a natural disaster. The New York *Times* remarked on the scene in an article entitled "Screams and Dreams in Times Square," while the New York *Post's* commentary was headed "'N Sync's Virgin Visit Prompts Teenybopper Frenzy."

And the frenzy didn't confine itself to the physical world; virtual pandemonium reined as well when it came to the 'N Sync five. The band's fans have set AOL records for chat participants, with close to 100,000 fans from all over the world jamming the e-waves to talk with their favorite band.

All bands prepare themselves for a grueling promotional tour to get the word out about a new album, but 'N Sync seemed tireless in the weeks surrounding the release of *No Strings Attached*. The guys took on TV appearances on MTV's *Total Request Live*, *Ultrasound*, *Snowed In*, and *Making the Video*; *Good Morning America*; *Saturday Night Live*; *The Tonight Show with Jay Leno*; *The Rosie O'Donnell Show*; *The View*; and even *Nickelodeon*.

Finally, after all the excitement and madness, the band retreated (well, 'N Sync-style retreating) to an undisclosed Manhattan venue for a night of celebrating at their very own album release party complete with mime artists and clowns. Special guests included Lisa "Left Eye" Lopes and Luther Vandross.

No Strings Attached lived up to all of the hype in a big way. In 'N Sync signature style, the album opens with the in-your-face hit "Bye Bye Bye" and delivers a twelve-song ride of the very best the band has to offer. With more sophisticated vocal stylings and a tougher, edgier sound, the band presents an altogether more experimental and confident 'N Sync. *No Strings* is a filler-free album, and picking standout tracks proved difficult for reviewers. "Space Cowboy (Yippie-Yi-Yay)" is a rousing dance track featuring TLC's own Lisa "Left Eye" Lopes. J.C. told *MTV News* January 27, 2000, that he thought it would "be cool to have a female's perspective on a male album. You got five guys on one record, and then just to throw a female perspective in there for a second to see what they're thinking about—it's cool. So we definitely decided she was the go-to. As far as female rappers, for her she was the go-to right away." The band brings Johnny Kemp's eighties hit "Just Got Paid" up to Y2K speed to great effect, making good use of their harmonizing skills hand-in-hand with that famous 'N Sync high energy. The last track added to the album, "It Makes Me Ill," features the signature sound of producer She'kspere (a.k.a. Kevin Briggs), the man behind TLC's "No Scrubs" and Destiny's Child's "Bills, Bills, Bills." 'N Sync breaks up the full-speed-ahead pace of the album beautifully with three ballads just crying out for a slow dance: Richard Marx's "This I Promise You," the Diane Warren-penned "That's When I'll Stop Loving You," and the a cappella "I Thought She Knew." Justin shares songwriting and producing credits on what *Billboard* dubbed "the deliciously old-school 'I'll Be Good For You,' with its soft shuffle beat and sweeping strings" in its March 25 review. The song is "about how I would treat a woman if I was in love with her," Justin told *Teen People* in its February 11, 2000, issue. "Like, 'I know the way I am is a bit overwhelming, but I want you to know that it's all from the heart.' That seems to be my problem with all my ex-girlfriends: I think I loved them too much from the very beginning. I found out girls need to chase a little." J.C. further whets his own writing and producing chops on "Space Cowboy," title track "No Strings Attached," "Bringin' da Noise," and the decidedly sexy "Digital Get Down."

And how about the guys themselves? What do they think of *No Strings Attached*? J.C. told *Billboard* in its February 14, 2000, edition, "The new album has a slightly different sound, more of an R&B edge, and more uptempo. We're just taking pop music to another level." Joey went on to elaborate that the band members "were given total control in the studio. We chose the songwriters and producers we wanted to work with. With this album, we are being completely true to ourselves." "It's our baby. This is like our first album, really," Lance revealed to *Entertainment Weekly Online* on January 31. "It's basically ourselves; we're doing it ourselves. We wrote and produced half of it. And the sound is way more edgy than the first album. It has a little bit more of a rock feel and a hip-hop feel to it. It's a real up-tempo, edgy, very pumped-up energetic album." "It's definitely nice to have some creative freedom and to really express ourselves," Justin says on the official 'N Sync web site. "But I think when you listen to this album in comparison to our debut album, you'll say to yourself that we took our sound to the next level." He also revealed his happiness with Jive Records to Roger Coletti of the MTV Radio Network on January 26, saying, "The thing that I love about our new record label, Jive, is that they're so open to our ideas. They don't shoot 'em down. Even at the tip-top, [Jive CEO] Clive Calder is so hands-on with us in A&R-ing this album. He's worked with us on it, and he's always asked us, 'What do you wanna do?' And that, you can't beat that." Lance put it simply in his September 1, 1999, Yahoo! Chat, saying, "We also feel finally free of what has been holding us back; we are in control of everything we do. Groups like us are usually all guided about and told what to do, and that is so not us. So we are here to tell you we have no strings attached."

What now? A little "R and R" for the boys? A well-deserved summer break? Some time to visit with friends and family, finish decorating their new digs, do a spot of sunbathing poolside, reflect on their success, and—as they say—rest on their laurels? Not a chance. This is 'N Sync we are talking about. As Johnny Wright raved to *Rolling Stone* in its March 30, 2000, issue, "This group has a work ethic like I've never seen. Usually at their level, they start saying, 'You're working me to death. I need more time to spend my money, more time to spend with my girl.' It's not like that with them." 'N Sync truly adores every aspect of their musical career, and they intend to make the most of it. The band is heading out on their biggest tour yet, which kick-starts May 9 in Biloxi, Mississippi, and carries on throughout the summer months.

And just in case performing to sold-out stadiums every night all across the country becomes a bit less than challenging, 'N Sync has a few extra-credit projects in the works. Of course, this is nothing new. The band had a cameo on the CBS television series *Touched by an Angel*, but that was just the beginning of 'N Sync's collective acting experiences. Another acting gig was a lingering leftover of the Pearlman connection in the form of the forthcoming Pearlman-produced movie, *Jack of All Trades*. Lance stars as a flight engineer, and the rest of the band has small roles in the film, due out in the summer of 2000. *Jack of all Trades* also features the acting prowess of Kenny Rogers, KC (of KC and the Sunshine Band fame), and none other than Britney Spears—who plays a flight attendant. Justin's major role in the Kathie Lee Gifford starring ABC television movie *Model Behavior* gave him an on-screen love interest in *Party of Five's* Maggie Lawson. Lance, meanwhile, took a dip in the acting pool himself, appearing on the January 31 episode of TV's *Seventh Heaven* in which he shares a kiss with cast member Beverley Mitchell. He described taping the smooch as "definitely not romantic" to *Entertainment Weekly Online* on January 31, explaining that "the whole time you're thinking about what you look like." "I was nervous," he admitted to *Teen People* in the magazine's February 11, 2000, issue. "It's a lot harder than people think, with fifty people watching you and cameras everywhere."

Justin has established the Justin Timberlake Foundation, a nonprofit organization set up to foster music and arts programs in schools. He told *Rolling Stone* in its March 30, 2000, issue, "I grew up in the boondocks, and there just wasn't a good musical program at school." He goes on to explain, very wisely for a nineteen-year-old, "I've thought about it a little bit—this and the whole Columbine incident. Music is another way for young minds and young bodies to express themselves, to find a way to get all those negative thoughts and energies out." Concern over the mindset of his peers has always been Justin's way; in November 1999 he joined up with professional athletes and students from various states at Boston's FleetCenter for the sixth annual Team Harmony, a daylong event of dialogue and education aimed at battling racism.